Until We See Your Smiling Face

A 21-Day Devotional

Betty Jean Poznak

Other books by Betty Jean Poznak:

Beloved Daughter Be Loved Daughter

Good Morning God, How Are You?

Beloved Friends Forever

I dedicate this book to God, who is my everything, this one is for You and to my late father John, who made me the tenacious warrior that I am. Thank you, Dad.

Acknowledgments

A special thanks to my editor and friend, Lynn Guttman Lent. I appreciate your time and for teaching me in the process of our editing.

Table of Contents

Introduction

Day One…A do over

Day Two…Guard our heart

Day Three… Forgiveness

Day Four…Acceptance

Day Five…How important is it?

Day Six…Slow down

Day Seven…Favorite seasons

Day Eight…Seek God

Day Nine… Play more

Day Ten…Admitting our struggles

Day Eleven…My ego is not my amigo

Day Twelve…Speak life

Day Thirteen…Celebrate

Day Fourteen…Self-care

Day Fifteen…Soul-care

Day Sixteen…Kingdom-care

Day Seventeen…Trust God

Day Eighteen…God's will

Day Nineteen…Friendships

Day Twenty…Abba time

Day Twenty-one…Beloved sons and daughters

Final thoughts

Final notes

Until We See Your Shining Face

Introduction

It takes anywhere from 18-254 days for a person to form a new habit and an average of 66 days for a new behavior. My hope is that this 21-day daily devotional will contribute to your already existing "toolbox" of gems or if you have not to this point read this type of format, it may begin a healthy routine of self-reflection, daily prayer and meditation for you. I pray that this daily reminder will be a companion to you and that it promotes a deeper relationship with Abba Father, which can be reread from the beginning on day one after the twenty-one days are complete. There are questions included that I encourage you to be intentional about and to take a few moments to answer; however, there are no right or wrongs, conditions or constraints, this sacred and valuable quiet time is

for you in any way you see fit.

Day One

Do over

This is the first day of the rest of your life! Sometimes we need a "makeover" and other times we need a complete "do over." You get to start again today, yesterday is gone, the present – this very moment is another shot at whatever it is that God put in your heart to do.

That dream, goal, or word that has been spoken over you to be triumphant and victorious is bursting forth for you to grab hold of.

What has been burning and searing inside of you to accomplish today? Doing it does it! It's just that simple. Make the effort and God will take care of the outcome. Faith without works is dead. Pray and take the action, if it is from God, there is nothing and no one that can stop it. Be intentional today.

What is it that gets you excited and brings you joy?

What has God put on your heart to do today?

What can you do today to start the process?

Verse for the day: Proverbs 16:3 NIV

"Commit to the Lord whatever you do, and he will establish your plans."

Additional thoughts

Day Two

Guard your heart

No matter how I feel today I won't allow my heart to lead me. Of course, I acknowledge and feel feelings. There is a lot to get sad about, fearful of, and stressed over. However, I won't allow those feelings of anxiety, worry, confusion, and disappointment to lead me today. I can feel emotions and ask God to help me with them. I can call a friend or a mentor. I can go for a walk and get out into nature and get some fresh air. I can make a gratitude list and thank God for everything that is going well and for what I do have. I can read the word of God and pray. Although I am of the thinking that what is denied cannot be healed, I also believe that if I allow those negative feelings to control what I say, think or do, I can go into dangerous territory. The safest place in the world I can be is in God's will and in his word; I am already in His heart. What does His word say about our hearts? He tells us to guard and watch over them. For out of it are the issues of life. Today I will be led by God and His word; I will not be guided by how I feel. Feelings aren't necessarily facts. The truth is in the Bible which never changes, does not need revisions or editing. When life alternating circumstances happen, we can halt, ask God to help us through it, and remember that He is always a "knee mail" away. We pause, breathe and simply call out on the one that knows us by name. The one who knows every hair on our head, the Creator who fiercely loves us and longs to father and protect us.

What is something you could turn over to God today that may be causing you pain, anxiety, or stress?

What emotions lead you at times?

What are some ways you can acknowledge and promptly get into God centered solutions?

Verse for the day: 1 Peter 5:7 NIV

"Cast all your anxiety on him because he cares for you."

Additional thoughts

Day Three

Forgiveness

Forgiveness is something that is life changing, it sets us free. When I forgive someone of an offense, I am not saying what happened was acceptable. I don't have to condone what happened. I don't even need to trust that person. If someone steals from me, I can pardon them, but I won't be leaving out my credit card either. When I hold onto a wrongdoing, I can become resentful, reliving the event repeatedly. Why on earth would I want to remind myself and recall a person and moment that caused me hurt and suffering? The sooner I wipe the slate clean, the quicker I am let out of the prison of being linked like a chain to them. I am called to be set apart and forgive. God knows the details and the whole story. I trust that He will vindicate me and heal those places that I have been wrong. I have also fallen short and have harmed others. In those instances, I can ask God to help me right my errors and injuries so that we all are set free and can move forward. It is difficult to be of service to God when I am shackled and attached to bitterness and bad memories. We can let go and walk free and celebrate what God has next for us to do. If The Almighty can forgive us of all our shortcomings, then so can we.

Is there someone you need to forgive today? If yes, who?

Is there someone you know that you could apologize to and ask for forgiveness?

Verse for the day: Colossians 3:13 NIV

"Bear with each other and forgive one another if any of you has a grievance against someone. Forgive as the Lord forgave you."

Additional thoughts

Day Four

Acceptance

Acceptance is not always approving or liking what is happening in our life. I don't always enjoy everything I see on the news, social media or even in my adult children's lives. But if I have learned anything, most things aren't any of my business. If my name isn't on it and I am not asked, who am I to give my two cents? I love being a peacemaker but sometimes I am called to pause and allow God to be God. Who do I think I am anyway? I surrender what I think people should be or what they should do. I focus on what is. I zero in on God knowing that He is more than capable. Today I will endorse and welcome what God brings my way. I know that the Almighty knows what He is doing. He has everything under control, He knows tomorrow's headlines and He sees around corners. Just for this moment I can relinquish my control trusting that it is in letting go that there is peace. The pain is in the holding on tightly to something or someone that I am not designed to carry. Suffering is in the resistance and lack of trust in God. I have the confidence and expectation that everything at this very moment is exactly the way it needs to be. I can relax and take it easy, breathe and thank God that His plan will be even better than our own undertaking.

What is something that you are holding onto that you could relinquish to God today?

If you knew that God could work it out better than you, would you release the situation?

How can you take the initiative right now to demonstrate that you do in fact trust God?

Verse for the day: Romans 8:28 NIV

"And we know that in all things God works for the good of those who love Him, who have been called according to His purpose."

Additional thoughts

Day Five

How important is it?

How important is it? Don't sweat the small stuff! I believe that most of what we get annoyed by won't even matter next month, let alone five years from now. Today we can enjoy every detail and every single moment. We will look for the good in people and in everything we see. When we are in traffic, it can give us the opportunity to pray for others. While sitting at another annoying red light, we can pray for a family member or a friend's prayer request. Perhaps we can go out for a walk and move a little slower and smile at a passerby. We can appreciate the birds and notice all the fine details of the trees, clouds and sky. We can be vigilant about observing whatever comes our way. We could call a friend and get out of ourselves. I have come to recognize that whatever I focus on becomes bigger, so instead of sweating the little things I can zero in on what is good. An attitude of gratitude goes a long way. All of us can take our concerns and disturbances and instead of being consumed and ravished by them, place them in our hands and just as we would release a butterfly from our palms, raise our arms in the air to God and let go, releasing what is troubling us. Today we can look for God in people, we can be a blessing not a burden. Today we will bless others and change our perspective because all is well in this very moment.

How major is what you are holding on to?

Who can you bless or do a good deed for someone today?

Verse for the day: 2 Corinthians 4: 8 NIV

"We are hard pressed on every side, but not crushed; perplexed, but not in despair."

Additional thoughts

Day Six

Slowdown

Somedays I need to hurry up and stop! I was always a Go-Go Girl. I only had one speed…faster. It took some injuries, accidents, and aging to realize that as much as I love being productive and motivated, I also need to slow down and smell the roses.

There is a time to go, and a time to pause; relaxing and resting isn't a weakness. Even athletes know when to recover from an injury or a taxing game. For an athlete resting is part of training.

Today I will allow myself some time to recline and rejuvenate. Even Jesus went up to the mountain alone to pray. I can go up on my "mountain" whether it's at a park, my bedroom, the beach, prayer closet, or onto my patio. I will set aside some time to meditate, be still, and pray. There is refreshment, healing, and renewing after some time out. Today I will mimic an athlete and allow my body and mind to get the adequate amount of rest and recovery.

Could you allow yourself some time out to recharge today?

Where can you go to be quiet for a few minutes and reflect?

Verse for the day: Mark 1: 35 KJV" And in the morning, rising up a great while before day, he went outt, and departed into a solitary place, and there prayed."

Additional thoughts

Day Seven

Favorite seasons

There is a time and season for everything. I happen to love the autumn with all its brilliant colors, a treasury of red, orange, bronze, gold and yellow foliage. I imagine inhaling the smell of apple cider, pumpkin pie loaded with homemade whipped cream and S'mores over a wood fire pit. (Who doesn't like a campfire?) This is the prime time and opportunity to wear a sweater or a favorite jacket because of the drop in temperature that invigorates and revitalizes us after a humid, and at times torrid summer. I envision a cup of steaming hot chocolate that I can pick up 'to go' from a nearby cafe that keeps my slightly chilled hands toasty. Perhaps we can seek out a local fall festival that offers tractor led hayrides and/or fun corn mazes for all levels. I imagine catching up on a fiction or nonfiction book that I've been meaning to read, while enjoying a coffee, latte or steaming hot tea in my favorite ceramic cup and perhaps I could add a pinch of pumpkin spice flavor for the harvest-time occasion, while curling up under my weighted blanket, dressed in my cozy sweatshirt, thick socks or favorite pajamas in the comfort of my home.

In my opinion fall is a time that tickles all our five senses which makes me cheerful and quite happy. Everyone has their favorite time of the year, each for their own set of reasons. Today we can ponder a joyful season or time, and if possible, take advantage of all its beauty, and possibilities. Whether it is taking a walk, hike or out for a scenic drive to observe and take in all its artistry and wonder, I encourage you to meditate on these things, because these are all of God's creations that He has blessed every one of us with. In my opinion our five senses will thank us and our hearts will rejoice in what God has created for all of us to enjoy. What are you waiting for? What time is it? THE TIME IS NOW!

What is your favorite season, and why?

Can you plan a trip or a vacation during your favorite time of year?

Where would you enjoy going ?

If you could not go to your desired destination, how could you replicate that same experience, and bring it into your own home?

Ecclesiastes 3:1 NIV

"There is a time for everything, and a season for every activity under the heavens."

Additional thoughts

Day Eight

Seek God

Have you ever lost or forgotten something in hopes of finding it? Last night I realized I forgot this manuscript up to this point at the library. I went to read what I had written thus far to my husband and discovered I hadn't brought it home. I prayed on and off through the night and even stayed up a bit concerned that I would not find it. But I called at 9:00 AM on the dot and when they opened, I walked into the library at 9:02. I asked several people at the front desk including the cleaning crew who came out and looked through the garbage with me after not finding it in the lost and found. I admit I cried like a baby as it looked quite grim. However, 30 minutes later the night crew found it in all of its glory intact and unharmed. I was so happy I hugged each of them and profusely thanked the staff as if I won a $1,000,000. I offered the employees a tip, but they graciously declined it. This notebook may not be a treasure of words to some people, but to me, it is my very heart and soul. Sometimes it's a pair of keys, sunglasses or a wallet that we misplace or fail to remember where we have placed them. When something is important or necessary, we will search high and low for it we will ask others for their help in some cases like I did this morning. What a relief when we find it. Can you imagine if we searched God out as intensely today as in those cases? The great news is all I need to do is seek God and He is there in a heartbeat. It doesn't take hours; He doesn't have an open or close time like the library. He is in our hearts; He is a whisper away. There are God incidences galore. I just need to open my eyes up and my mind to His glorious presence. He is alive and well in you and in everyone we meet today. Thankfully He never gets lost, but I admit I do misplace where He belongs at times. I pray that today I keep him first and foremost in my day and in my life. May others spot Him when they see me and you today. Allow God to be visible and in view when they are around you. Our pursuit and quest for the Lord always brings about a discovery of a lifetime.

Have you lost or misplaced something important recently that you found?

How did it affect you?

If you sought God as intensely how would that improve your relationship with him?

Verse for the day: Deuteronomy 4;29 an NIV
"But if from there you seek the Lord your God, you will find Him if you seek Him with all your heart and with all your soul."

Additional thoughts

Day Nine

Play more

Life is serious and at times quite demanding. We have great responsibilities and people who depend on us. However, we need to take time to have fun and enjoy our hobbies and interests outside of our workdays. I must admit I need to try these days, to have more playtime. We are not created to be glum and solemn 24/7. There is a time to labor and a time to enjoy recreation. My husband is a sports enthusiast, he loves soccer, football and basketball. He has watched hundreds of games on television, and I enjoyed watching his passion when his team won. There is great joy when we partake in our hobbies and recreation. I enjoy running, hiking and worship music where I can dance unto the Lord. When I take the time to engage in these activities, I am a happy lady. As children we played often. I want to encourage you to have some social time or to enjoy a craft or sport today. We work hard so why not play hard?

What can you do today that is fun?

What hobby or pastime comes to mind that you can add to your day?

Verse for the day: Ecclesiastes 8:15 NLT
"So, I recommend having fun, because there is nothing better for people in this world than to eat, drink, and enjoy life. That way they will experience

some happiness along with all the hard work God gives them under the sun."

Additional thoughts

Day Ten

Admitting our struggles

Addictions are prevalent now more than ever, whether it is to food, alcohol, drugs, internet, social media, performance, work or to people. Dependency and cravings are no joke. I remember being asked to write the pros and cons of my obsession to alcohol and what I came up with was staggering and eye opening. I had two pros for drinking, I danced better, and I was less self-conscious with the opposite sex. The cons took up a full page. I lost my morals, values and belief system. I felt disconnected from my first love God. I blacked out and got into trouble. The negative consequences went on and on. It's one thing to think on these things it's a whole other to see it in black and white. I was sick and tired of being sick and tired, the gig was up. I finally surrendered and went into a treatment center and a 12-step program. Soon after I realized I also had an addiction to food and exercise. I wrote another list of pros and cons and like the former list, I saw a similar common denominator, a couple of pros but many more liabilities. Truth be told it wasn't what I was eating but what was eating at me. That I explained in the book 'Beloved Daughter Be Loved Daughter' in great length and detail. If something is more important than God, we need to remove it from the top of the list, some people have balance and moderation, my hat is off to you. Thank God that this is not an issue for you. You can pray for those of us who do struggle. But if we are completely honest, I believe there are times we may wrestle with habits or weaknesses that we could ask for help with and surrender once and for all. It takes a lot of guts and courage to say I need help and quite frankly, I do.

Is there anything that you are dependent on or see an unhealthy habit forming?

What are the pros and cons of this dependency or characteristic ?

Are you willing to ask for help? What does that look like to you?

Verse for the day: Proverbs 14:16 NLT

"The wise are cautious and avoid danger; fools plunge ahead with reckless confidence."

Additional thoughts

Day Eleven

My ego isn't my amigo

Humility is something I aspire to. Simply put, humility isn't thinking less of ourselves but thinking of our self-less often. Dying to self and thinking about others isn't always easy or convenient. If I am honest, there were countless times I did put others ahead of me and I enjoyed their recognition and accolades Humility doesn't show off or need applause. When I do a good deed or something nice for someone it can be between us and God. I don't need to perform for a crowd or tell anyone. That is my ego and pride that needs to be stroked. My ego isn't always my amigo. Humility keeps me rightsized. We all have talents, and we all have weaknesses. Being able to say I need help, or I don't know isn't a shortcoming. In my opinion it's the bravest thing I can do. Speaking up for myself and saying I can't do this alone takes courage. I needed to say I need help many times and didn't and it only hurt me and kept me stuck. Whenever anyone has asked me for help, and it was in my power to do so, it felt amazing. It brought me joy to be of service to another human being. Why would I want to deny another person that same happiness and joy that I experienced when I assisted someone? It can be as simple as opening a door for someone, volunteering at church to be a greeter or making coffee at a 12-step meeting. We are not an island; we need each other and if it's in our power to help we do so. If we need a turn, we take it. I believe we are all teachers some days and students on others. Jesus taught us in the beatitudes that God blesses those who are humble, for they will inherit the whole earth. I listen to Jesus, and I believe him, he is the best example of humility. There was no ego, pride or arrogance in his character, quite the contrary. Jesus oozes humility, service, love and mercy. There is no favoritism or status. We are all the same at the foot of the cross. We can come as we are. God doesn't desire anything except my heart and communication with Him. He wants me to hunger and thirst after righteousness and not after "fillers" that never truly complement our life. Nothing in this world can satisfy us but God. Abba is enough and if we can live from that truth, we will have peace and harmony with God, others and ourselves like never before.

What does humility mean to you?

Is there someone you can help today?

Is there something you can ask assistance with?

Verse for the day: Ephesians 4: 2 NIV

"Be completely humble and gentle; be patient, bearing with one another in love."

Additional thoughts

Day Twelve

Speak life

Speak life! No matter how I feel or what I see I can trust that God's words in His love letters to us are true. We have the power of God inside all of us and can activate His power by speaking the Bible out loud. Words are powerful, they can bless God and people and ourselves, but they can also curse and keep us stuck. We already have everything we need whether it's our health, our daily bread or strength to overcome something monumental. We only need to declare it out loud and use the words that the Old and New Testaments proclaim. What we say matters, I want to be an encourager and a supporter of others. I wish to be iron sharpening iron and cheer others on. That doesn't mean I always agree with someone or their lifestyle. We are here to spur each other on in the faith of God and all we put our hand to. It may take effort and some work, but when we practice it becomes more natural.

We can get excited about our favorite sports teams and shout out "way to go" and high five each other when a player scores or makes an awesome play. Why not be as passionate about the people God places in our lives and applaud our fellow traveler for their gifts, talents and most importantly, for being a brother or sister in Christ? It is easy to be critical and to focus on other people's shortcomings but that doesn't benefit others like a kind word will. I am not saying we can't be honest if someone asks us our point of view. I am simply suggesting that in my opinion having others supporting me and my growth, encouraging my endeavors is much more effective than shaming me or judging me. We are all in this game together. Let's find the best place for each of us and play our hearts out on this team called life.

Are you typically an encourager? Explain.

Is there someone you can acknowledge today and speak a kind word to?

If so, who?

Which scripture can you read that would assist you in speaking life?

Verse for the day: 1 Thessalonians 5:11 NIV

"Therefore encourage one another and build each other up, just as in fact you are doing."

Additional thoughts

Day Thirteen

Celebrate

Celebrating holidays and people's birthdays are a highlight for many of us. But I know for some folks it can be a challenging time. I want to encourage you the next time there is an anniversary, birthday or celebration, to partake in it like you never have before. If that means hosting a gathering or creating a personal card or a thoughtful gift, let's be involved in the festivities.

We host Thanksgiving in our home often and I find it joyful to have family over visiting us. I am not the greatest cook, though I do try and have greatly improved with the help of my spouse. I sure do enjoy breaking bread with my husband, children and extended family members.

There is always someone or something to celebrate. We have time markers for friends in a recovery program who are recognizing a year of sobriety or multiple years. Perhaps we can acknowledge a friend who may be receiving a job promotion or pay raise.

And what about Christmastime when many of us recline around the green pine tree which is decorated with garland, candy canes, personable ornaments that hang from the branches and topped with a glistening star. A manger which is placed underneath the scented six-foot beauty, front and center, reminding us we are remembering the birth of Jesus Christ and not just a season of gift giving.

Celebrating people and anniversaries are the perfect moment to try different restaurants or to attempt something fun or to plan on traveling to a new town, city or destination. We are not a glum group; we are created to work hard and to play hard. I also need to mention that I think it is perfectly fine to let others know when we are celebrating a birthday or a milestone. People aren't mind readers. I have no qualms about informing my friends and inviting them out for a lunch or over to my house to celebrate me too. Not in an egotistical or pompous way but being openly and modestly available to observe me like I would others. We have a lot of responsibilities and routines; I think it's great to balance those times out with a party, holiday or acknowledgement of a milestone.

Is there someone that you know getting ready to celebrate a birthday or milestone?

What can you do to offer or contribute to the celebration?

Is a holiday coming up that you can try something new to have more joy or participation in?

What will you do?

Verse for the day: Proverbs 15 :15 NLT
"For the despondent every day brings trouble, for the happy heart, life is a continual feast."

Additional thoughts

Day Fourteen

Self-care

Doing something nice for ourselves is at times on the bottom of our list of priorities. However, it is important to have self-care. Taking time to pray and meditate gives us a spiritual boost. Going for a walk, hiking, running or lifting weights improves our health and well-being. I always feel better after I partake in 30 to 60 minutes of exercise. I love the colors of flowers and their scents. I can pick a few from the garden or go out and purchase a bouquet and display them in a lovely vase where I can see them in my home. (My husband is famous for doing that for me). Spending time with friends and family is a way to experience joy. Getting my hair done or having a manicure /pedicure is a way of treating myself well. Attending the theater, an art gallery or concert is a treat. Also listening to music, writing and journaling are simple pleasures. We all have our likes and dislikes it doesn't matter what it is that you enjoy, just do something.

I want to encourage you today to choose at least one thing that you can do for yourself that would put a smile on your face and promote kindness towards you. There are many of us who are pretty good at loving our neighbors, but we feel selfish and self-centered about giving to ourselves. Even Jesus said to love others as yourself, which in my opinion implies we are to love ourselves as well; it is a given.

What can you do for yourself today that would be loving?

Do you believe that you are as important as others?

Verse for the day: Galatians 5: 14 NIV

"For the entire law is fulfilled in keeping this one command: love your neighbor as yourself."

Additional thoughts

Day Fifteen

Soul-care

Soul care is another way of saying self-care, but whatever you choose to name it, I think that it is caring for our inner selves that matters greatly. Do we care enough about God's masterpiece, the temple He gave to each of us? His home is in our hearts and inner being. He resides in our body, and we can make Him feel comfortable and cozy or we can at times put invisible signs up all around us that read 'caution', 'no trespassing' or 'stay out'. We do that simply by building walls around us or bringing the wrong things into our sanctuary. How about we make our sacred place and inner sanctum a location that speaks life, love and safety. A banner that blares "welcome home, come on in and stay." When I visualize Abba coming home inside of my soul, I yearn to feed Him nourishing foods, and placing Him in the best chair in the house, wishing for Him to rest and to feel warmth and comfort as He reclines. I offer Him a drink and ask if there is anything I can get for him. It's a beautiful request and exchange. Now I ask you what would sustain your vitality today? I encourage us to attend to our souls because we will also be showing up and visiting God himself. We have invited the Creator to come into our hearts and our life. We have requested that our Savior forgives us for our shortcomings. He not only forgives us, but He also forgets it. Never to be brought up again.

When we have self-care and soul care, we also have cared for God. May the Almighty always feel greeted, taken in and accepted into our dwelling place which is our earthly residence until the day we go on to our permanent home in Heaven.

How can you display soul and self-care in the next 24 hours?

How can we welcome God into our home and interbeing?

Verse for the day 1 Corinthians 3:17 NIV
"If anyone destroys the temple, God will destroy that person; for God's temple is sacred and you together are that temple."

Additional thoughts

Day Sixteen

Kingdom-care

Yesterday we covered soul care, today let's pour into Kingdom care.

They will know we are Christians by our love. We don't need to announce or flaunt it we do it quietly. The Bible says in Matthew 6:3, "But when you give to someone in need, don't let your left hand know what your right hand is doing."

We are called to love out loud but not loudly. What does that mean, everything we do either glorifies and honors God or it doesn't. It's not rocket science, we complicate it. God makes it clear to love him with all our hearts, souls and minds and to love others as ourselves. That is in my opinion, Kingdom care. We all have our own talents, gifts and parts of the body that help the other members. My pastor

Peggy has the gifts of teaching and pastoral shepherding and many more, I am sure. My husband has the gifts of teaching, hospitality and praying. I believe after many years in ministry and several assessments and gift tests that I completed, I lean towards encouraging, faith and showing mercy. There are several different spiritual gift tests we can Google on the web sites and are free for the taking. I found it helpful to assess where I may be most helpful to God and others. As much as I enjoy watching my pastor preaching, I would feel more comfortable speaking about my testimony, how God has restored me and how I have overcome a slew of addictions and traumas than preaching from a pulpit. Her calling is not mine and vice versa. I need my pastor to lead with godly counsel and to interpret biblical scripture for our congregation. Of course, we can all read the word and research ourselves as well but one of the reasons I go to my congregation is for my shepherd to teach and preach sound traditional doctrine. Her caring and wise, thought-out messages charge me to become closer to God, to be obedient to His word and to love others both within the walls of our building and out in all my affairs. I couldn't preach like she does nor am I called to do so. I am still part of one body, just as the arms don't function the same as the brain does. Each member of our physical body operates differently, but we need each one to perform its duty in order to be 100%. Thank God our body isn't made up of only an eye, we would look creepy. Or if we had one mouth, we sure would talk even more most likely. Ha! So just as importantly, our body in Christ needs to be orderly and each taking its role so we can be healthy and operational. Could you imagine if everyone had the gift of administration? We would all be governing and leading each other and there would be no one to help or serve. We need the organizers and planners but like our body, we don't want to be one giant eye or one giant delegator. Kingdom care is knowing what your gifts and talents are and then going out and manifesting them into all you do. We serve and come under God asking, " Thy will be done on earth as it is in heaven." Not one gift is superior, higher ranked or better than another. We need all of them to function properly. As much as the heart is essential to surviving so is the liver, kidneys and brain. We need every single part. If you are called to evangelize, give, heal, pray in the spirit or prophesy , do it all unto the Lord and do it for Him alone. Not to be applauded or to be recognized but simply because we are all called to do so. It's perfectly fine to shine and to stand out and be set apart, I find that it comes naturally. But let that be from God who lifts us up and not ourselves who couldn't even do what we do without God's breath that He alone has breathed into us. Lastly, remember that God doesn't always call the equipped but instead will at times equip the called.

Which gifts can you use today to be of service to both God and others?

What are your spiritual gifts?

If you are unsure of your gifts, can you research the internet and find a Spiritual Gifts Test to download or go to your local church to print one out and simply answer the survey to get started?

What can you do today to help another person and not be found out?

If you are already serving and ministering to God and others my hat is off to you, we need you, I need you. Keep up the great works of God.

Verse for the day Romans 12:3-8 KJV

"For I say, through the grace given unto me, to every man that is among you not to think of himself more highly than he ought but to think soberly according as God hath dealt to every man the measure of faith. For as we have many members in one body and all members have not the same office so we being many are one body in Christ and everyone members one of another. Having then gifts differing according to the grace that is given to us, whether prophecy, let us prophesy according to the proportion of faith, or ministry, let us wait on our ministering or he that teaches on teaching, or he that exhorted us on exhortation that with diligence he that showeth with mercy, with cheerfulness."

Additional thoughts

Day Seventeen

Trust God

Trusting God completely is one of the greatest complements that we can give to our Father. Stepping out of ourselves and laying down our concerns at the feet of our Abba says, "I trust you." I surrender, I know that You can be trusted with all of me. All that I am and all that I have belongs to Him. My dog, Cinnamon follows me around the house constantly. If I am sitting at the kitchen table writing, she is by my feet. When I go to the couch, she plants herself on her ultra-plush bed next to me and looks up hoping for a stroke on the head and lots of petting. When we retire at night, she sleeps by our bedroom door. Her loyalty and trust in our family is heartwarming and pure innocence. She knows that when she is hungry, someone will feed her. If she needs to go outside to do her business, one of us lets her outside and takes her for a leisurely walk. My 75-pound redcoat companion knows without a shadow of a doubt that I love her, and in return I know that she loves and trusts me to take care of her. It's an unspoken language and expectation, it's a given. When we completely surrender and let go of trying to control, fix, figure things out and relinquish what we think things should look like or how things should be and trust Abba to work things out, we are then able to experience peace that passes all understanding. We just need to step out in faith, holding nothing back and at times even stepping out of complete pitch darkness knowing without a shadow of a doubt that the Lord is in complete and total control of everything and everyone at every second of every single day every single time.

I love the story about Mother Teresa and John Kavanagh. When John Kavanagh the noted and famous ethicist went to Calcutta, he was seeking Mother Teresa and more. He went for three months to work at the House of the Dying to find out how best he could spend the rest of his life. When he met Mother Teresa, he asked her to pray for him. "What do you want me to pray for?" she replied.

He then uttered the request he had carried thousands of miles, "Clarity. Pray that I have clarity."

" No", Mother Teresa answered, "I will not do that." When he asked her why she said, "Clarity is the last thing you are clinging to and must let go of." When Kavanaugh said that she always seemed to have clarity, the very kind of clarity he was looking for,

Mother Teresa laughed and said, "I have never had clarity; what I always had is trust. So, I will pray that you trust God."

When we can have that sink into our marrow, bones and heart, everything changes. Desiring clarity, we attempt to abolish the prospect of trusting God. Trepidation and angst of the unknown, trail sprawled ahead of us thus obliterating and demolishing any innocence like my dog Cinnamon exudes. It is the masters greatness and unrelenting tenderness and friendship that cements that kind of trust. Job from the Old Testament had that kind of unwavering trust too. I have had moments as well; I admit I have also taken my will back many times and I have paid for it dearly. It is when I look back on God's track record and see that it is perfect, 100% of the time, that I can once again breathe in and breathe out and remind myself," hey, God is love, kind, good, merciful, sovereign, almighty, powerful, holy, tender, a gentleman, kind and Omnipresent. He is Elohim, Yahweh, Our Creator, Jehovah Jireh our provider, Jehovah Shalom the Lord of peace, Redeemer, Shepherd, Glory of Israel, the Holy One of Israel. The God of Abraham, the King of Kings and Lord of Lords. Why wouldn't I trust him to take care of my family and everything else that concerns me?

Do you trust God?

How can you start trusting the Lord or continue to put your total trust in Abba today?

Verse for the day Proverbs 3: 5

"Trust in the Lord with all thine heart; and lean not unto thine own understanding."

Additional thoughts

Day Eighteen

God's will

Have you ever had a friend or family member say and do whatever you want? You ask them where they would like to go for dinner.

"Whatever you want is fine," they reply.

You ask them what are they in the mood for?

And they smile from ear to ear. "Oh, I'm not fussy, I can eat whatever you decide on, you go ahead and pick what we eat and where we go."

Could you imagine having that kind of dialogue with our Father?

Lord, I want whatever you want. I'm not particular or emotionally high maintenance. I can do whatever you choose and decide for me. You go ahead, Lord, and select what you want me to eat, have me do anything you request and take me where you desire me to go. We would not need to convince God about what our life should look like. He would instead get to convince us of a plan that supersedes our aspirations and game plans.

That takes trust, faith and maturity. When we walk with God and stay close by his side, we learn to depend and rely on him. It isn't codependent or unhealthy, quite the contrary. The more attached to God we are, the more confident and hopeful we become in all our comings and goings. We can have faith and assurance that God will only take us and do with us what is His perfect will. He is always by our side and will never leave or forsake us. As mentioned in my first book, 'Beloved Daughter Be Loved Daughter,' when my boys were babies and I would strap them into their car seats in the back of my then Volvo, I jumped into the driver's seat and placed my foot on the pedal, tapped the accelerator lightly, taking off for the next destination.

My boys did not start a riot act of questions. "Where are we going mommy? What are we doing? What's going on? Why are you going this way?" No, they simply sat back, enjoyed the ride and knew like always that I was taking them somewhere that they would be safe and enjoy. They trusted me and had an innocent dependence on me.

Could you envision that kind of exchange with God?

"Alright God, strap me in and wherever you transport us I am along for the ride. Wow, look at those beautiful trees that we are passing, and that vast blue sky is limitless. The window glides slowly down an inch and the cool crisp fresh air hits our face and we giggle like my toddlers would in a similar moment.

As we drive, the blood red sunset is taking its time at first and without warning it disappears, darkening the once expansive blue sky introducing a crescent moon. We marvel at God's creation, His wondrous tour, an excursion. All we need to do is sit back and enjoy the trip. No questions asked, we have faith that wherever our Father is taking us we will be safe and cared for. We are protected from danger, yes of course there is danger in life, but God is our shield, our seat belt. He guards and shelters us. He steers the wheel better than any professional driver or chauffeur and he takes us on a voyage of a lifetime. Buckle up, beloved sons and daughters, our handler is patiently waiting for us to sit back and enjoy this journey called life. So raise your full cup and make a toast, "L'chaim -to life!"

How can you have a childlike faith and trust in God today?

Do you try to convince God to do what you want Him to do?

Are you willing to allow God to convince you instead?

What does that look like to you?

Verse for the day Matthew 18: 3 TPT

"Learn this well: unless you dramatically change your way of thinking and become teachable like a little child, you will never be able to enter in."

Additional thoughts

Day Nineteen

Friendships

Thank God for friends, they are perfectly imperfect people just like me. I have many people I am surrounded by because of all the different activities I am involved in. Between the church, health club, organized runs and races, recovery programs, book clubs etc., I am very grateful and blessed to be encircled by like-minded people who want to grow and deepen their relationships with God and are equally yoked brothers and sisters. With that being said, there are a select few that know all the details of my heart and life. It's important to guard our hearts and at the same time be brutally honest about ourselves. I am positive I have some blind spots and don't see my shortcomings all the time, just ask my husband. In those instances, I need my mentors and accountability partners who are also my dear friends. We all need at least one or two intimate sisters or brothers who we can bounce our ideas off whom we can share dreams and our goals.

We don't always see what's best for us. Of course, I go to the Lord first and pray, meditate and/or fast, I believe that is paramount and most important. I am also mature enough to recognize that there is great wisdom in seeking godly direction in council. As the TPT version of the Old Testament says in Proverbs 27: 17 "It takes a grinding wheel to sharpen a blade and so one person sharpens the character of another." In other words, iron sharpens iron. It is necessary to refine and polish up all the darker and enlightened places inside of us. There are times we can become dim and inky and that is perfectly fine for a season. Not every day is rainbows, lollipops and skipping in the air. We aren't called to be fake, counterfeit or a sham. We all have moments of lying low and like Jesus going up onto a mountain to be still and prayerful with His father, our fellow Deity. It's a balancing act.

A spiritual advisor, counselor or devoted friend can offer advice and direction in any given situation or plan. During my life, I have done things without guidance and have paid for it dearly. When I reach out and ask for help or I can take a few minutes of someone's valuable time, I fare much better. There is victory and success when I call my "go to" girlfriends. My mentor and close friend Eileen has always prayed with me and for me and allows me to reason things out and talk things through, sometimes processing my own answers as we speak. My pastors and friends Peggy and Karen can discern the truth from the false and in doing so depart Biblical wisdom and clarity on the situations that I bring to them. There are also times I can receive wisdom from their messages on the pulpit Sunday mornings and Wednesday evenings and when we pray together. I would be remiss to leave out my best friend in the world who also shares my DNA and maiden name, Barbie. Although we are 14 months apart it is as though we were born identical twins. We can just look at each other and finish one another's sentence that is how bonded we are. We all need those companions who are invested in our spiritual health, personal growth and assisting in our comprehensive development and maturity. I believe it is imperative to live life fully. It doesn't hurt if they happen to be your cheerleader, but personally if I am dying, I don't care if you're an encourager or a naysayer, please just give me the truth and the facts. We all need accuracy and correction at times, it's imperative to be principled. I try to say what I mean, mean what I say and not to say it mean. I have quite a few realists in my circle, and I don't mind that they don't mince words with me, constructive modification and alternation removes unnecessary layers of bad habits and character defects. There have been seasons of friendships and a variety of types of rapport, some have been oak trees full of wisdom, honor, nobility and stability for me. To you the names Jenn, Barbie and Mary are just that titles, and a designated bunch of letters. We all have our own fill-in-the-blanks that come to mind.

If you were told you were going to die tomorrow, who would you call to tell?

Currently, we have a few platforms where we can share such news. But who would you call to inform of this huge news? Those are the 100 feet, 150-width solid oaks who have been withstanding incredibly strong storms, yes, the resilient people. We have them in our lives, God willing, and I would bet that you are one of those sturdy powerful life- affirming confidants too. What a beautiful compliment to have and be a symbol of such beauty and fortitude.

My late father (God rest his soul) used to write me letters when I left home at the tender age of 17 a few months after I graduated from high school in Lancaster, PA. In one of the sealed envelopes I received by him, was a beautifully written note that included a quote by an anonymous author, "There are good ships and wood ships, ships that sail the sea, but the best ships are friendships. May they always be."

My dad was my friend too.

My boys who are now adults are always going to be my juniors but there are glimpses of moments that they are also my buddies. My furball friend cinnamon is fiercely loyal and devoted to me. In fact, she is laying here next to me as I write this manuscript looking up at me with those puppy eyes that have glanced up at me thousands of times for the last 10 years of her 12 years of existence. She has heard an earful many a day from me, my husband and the boys. Those of you with pets know exactly what I am talking about. There are also those friends who you laugh with and giggle about everything and of absolutely nothing with. I have those ladies that we can just look at each other and start cracking up, they bring out the playful and silly side, no fair-weathered friends here, only playmates and comrades in life and in recreation. We all have those fun and zany friends who we can cry with, laugh with and call at any time for any reason. I have been blessed with a handful of pals. Whenever I am wanting to go out for lunch for a time of deep conversation or a simple catch up, I call Lori, Nanci, Pam or Leigh. We usually go for a walk and talk about everything from A-Z or break bread together and smile about all our accomplishments, our families and our feelings. I know that if I ever needed a shoulder to cry on, these women would be there for me in a heartbeat and vice versa. Why do I know that? Because they have. Intimacy into you I see, and into me you see. It's a beautiful pact. We know not to ever put anyone on a spiritual pedestal because we all fall short. Only Yeshua was flawless and without fault. I will be forever grateful that Jesus is always available 24 hours a day seven days a week, holidays included, with no conditions and no strings attached, he is a whisper away. How lovely and reassuring knowing that we are never alone. He is our constant companion. I think of him placing his tender but strong hands on my face, pulling me gently towards him, hugging me tenderly and kissing the top of my forehead and whispering, "Well done my good and faithful servant" Oh, what a glorious moment that will be, all because I asked him into my heart and life. We are dearly loved and fiercely liked. We are radically and deeply wanted. He is dying to be with us, the very thought of that kind of devotion brings me to joyful tears, we are all one day closer to that red carpet moment. I can't wait, but I will until he calls me home, until that celebration.

I want to encourage all of us to love without reservations, boundaries or barriers. Those friends we thought of just a moment ago, embrace them with a letter, call, text, date, gift or a kind word spoken over them. We all need more affection and happiness. In my opinion we can't out love anyone, there is always more room for additional love. Right now, take a moment and visualize Jesus reaching out and holding your hand, and in the other hand take hold of one of your closest friends. There are now no hands left to self-destruct or to harm another. Instead, there is an unshakable bond that supports us in all that we do. We need the Lord, and we need people. My friends have been God with skin on for me many times. Like Moses, our peeps can lead us towards the Promised Land, and like Mary Magdalen and the Virgin Mary who supported Jesus with their strength, let us emulate our predecessors and exude this kind of pact and inseparable bond.

Who are the ones you would call tomorrow if it was going to be the day you went to Heaven?

Who are your oak trees in life?

What are some experiences you have had with these people that have bonded you with them?

Who can you reach out to today for accountability in a matter that you are seeking clarity and discernment in?

Which constant friend can you bless today and how?

Verses for the day proverbs 11: 14 KJV

Where no counsel is, the people fall: but in the multitude of counselors there is safety.

Proverbs 27: 9 NIV

Perfume and incense bring joy to the heart, and the pleasantness of a friend springs from their heartfelt advice.

Proverbs 18: 24 KJV

"A man that hath friends must show himself friendly: and there is a friend that sticketh closer than a brother."

Additional thoughts

Day Twenty

Abba time

Prayer simply put is a conversation with God. As much as I favor the Lord's prayer in Luke 11: 2-4 because it was taught by Jesus, I also feel drawn to the Saint Francis prayer of Assisi. Every time I read it aloud or silently to myself, I get choked up. It is such a selfless and self-sacrificing invocation. The serenity prayer may be short, but it is sweet, and powerful in a moment where we may need some relief, calm or need to settle down. All of these are helpful petitions to the Lord, but it doesn't always need to be formal or traditional. Just as we would call a friend to talk, we can call out to our Father in Heaven and say anything and everything that's in our heart and on our minds. It can be as plain as please help me or thank you for another day alive. If you are a man or woman of few words, no problem if they are spoken, it's a prayer and God loves hearing from us. If you are a boy or girl who is known to pontificate and can babble for hours, I bet God doesn't mind at all. I don't know about you, but I could listen to my boys talk to me anytime for as long as they want. I wonder if God gets a kick out of us with some of our conversations. I talk to the Lord all day and night, about every single detail as though He was sitting next to me, whether in the car, at the dinner table or in bed. I can become quite chatty with Abba. I try daily to make a point in addition to fluid chitchat with him to also set aside a few minutes to ask for forgiveness for my sins and shortcomings. I have a list and even though He already knows them even better than me, confessing them out loud keeps me in check and humble. I spend a few moments praising God for being kind, loving, sovereign, holy, a gentleman, powerful and my friend. I speak the scripture I memorized from Psalms 100: 5 NIV "The Lord is good and his love indoors forever; his faithfulness continues through all generations." Followed by interceding for others and their needs. After a few requests I thank God for all my blessings including my husband, boys, sobriety, health, family, friends, home, dog, business, etc. I can't be hateful when I am grateful. Then I sing one of my favorite songs to the most high called 'I love you Lord and I lift my voice.' Most days I sing it to myself or quietly but occasionally I will play the Latria modern worship on YOUTUBE, and I lift my right hand in the air and with my left-hand touch above my chest to the very place my heart beats. Music and worship stir my soul and like David in the Psalms I have a heart for God and through dancing and belting out a course I feel an intimacy with Papa that I can only get with Him. Thankfully it doesn't matter that my vocals aren't too pleasant to the human ear. The word doesn't say sing beautifully it just says sing! Over and over, dozens of times we're commanded to sing to the Lord, sing praises, sing joyfully sing an old or new song. Like David which means beloved just belt one out. I believe it is music to God's ears when we worship and praise Him musically inclined or not. A conversation wouldn't be complete without closing my mouth for a moment. And that's how I end my date with God, I take some time with silence and meditation, it is my turn to zip it and to listen to what the Lord has to say. Sometimes it's a thought, vision, a person He puts on my heart or a picture or a story of Jesus. It may be that if I'm outside witnessing the sunrise, sunset, beach or mountains. Every encounter is different, but one thing is certain I always feel my Father's presence and His peace cascading over me, flooding me with love, peace, joy, patience, kindness, faithfulness, gentleness and self-control for the coming hours before I retire in the evening. So, whether we take an allotted time to acknowledge God or merely say, "Hi God it's me!" and chit chat away.

I believe that God loves hearing from us, all we need to be is real and honest. God created mankind in his own image. He could have stopped at the animals, but he chose to create male and female and to bless us. He even said in Genesis 1:31 "It was very good."

I believe that God loves us, likes us, desires us and is fond of you and me. I think the Lord longs for our devotion and affection everyday all day. I have never spent time with God and regretted it. It takes discipline and self-control to quiet the mind and to be still in the confidence that we will hear and listen to God's voice. But it is worth it every single time that I cease all other activities and lift my heart up to the King of Kings, the Lord of Lords and lean into his chest the very place that beats for you and me and to allow him to take great delight in us, and to rejoice over us with singing. (Zephaniah 3: 17)

What are some of your favorite prayers?

Are you pleased with your dates and time with God and if so, why?

Could you spend more quiet time with the Lord?

If so, can you pencil in sometime this week?

How do you worship and praise God?

Can you take a moment right now to have a little chat with God?

Is there a song you could sing whether it's a melody from your youth or something you invented yourself?

Verses for the day Psalms 32: 11 NIV

"Rejoice in the Lord and be glad, you righteous sing all you who are upright in heart!"

1 Thessalonians 5: 16-18 KJV

" Rejoice evermore. Pray without ceasing. In everything give thanks: for this is the will of God in Christ Jesus concerning you."

Additional thoughts

Day Twenty-one

Beloved sons and daughters

The Rabbi, Emmanuel isn't expecting us to be perfect, only authentic. When I reveal myself to Abba, he doesn't disown me. All my inadequacies, insecurities, fears, disappointments, hurts, dreams and desires are received and understood. Getting real with God is a gift. He knows everything about us anyway, but if we can get out of our own way and rise from self-deception, denial and disillusionment, He can then restore and heal those old coping skills and self-defeating patterns. We don't need to come to God perfect, good or as a saint. God doesn't love us because of what we do or don't do, God loves all of us because of who He is. God is love. When we can truly get that inside our bones and marrow we can live from a place of great gratitude and humility. How many times have I performed for God, people and even myself, sometimes unknowingly and other occasions quite aware that the accolades, pat on the back and applause for being a helper, server and good Christian girl are lurking in the background, bless my heart. I love that I have a heart for God, but I must always be brutally honest with God and me, why am I doing this next project or action? Is it to glorify and honor God alone or is there some ulterior motive such as recognition and bonus points? Many of us have servant hearts and we are givers. In my opinion that is a gift from God. But when we start to showcase or expect a standing ovation for our performance, humility has lost its luster. God wants to know us, the raw, real and actual us. We are safe in God's eyes, in his heart and

in his estimation of us. He created us, he breathed life into us. Why do we think that we must suit up and show up perfectly and glue a smile on our sometimes-weary faces? I love being happy, joyous and free but there are times that life happens, and we face some tragic news that obliterates our hearts and faith, and situations and people that broadside us. I don't think God is expecting us in these circumstances to skip and jump up and down with a forced smile when we're hurting. The shortest verse in the Bible is
" Jesus wept."

I have found when there is death, divorce, health issues or a loss and that I am real with my human emotions, God comforts me and tenderly embraces me. All we need to do is retreat and to get quiet, whether we are at home, at work, a park, the beach or away on a mountain just like Jesus would go to for his solitude and prayer. We can lay it all out at His feet and blast down the walls around us from all the spiritualizing, psychobabble, and theatrical perfectionism, we shatter and demolish the barricades that bind us allowing them to form a bridge that extends towards our Comforter and Patient Savior. God isn't looking for celebrity Christians, I'm speaking to myself as well, trust me. I can take responsibility and admit to God and to you that I crave approval, love and your acceptance at times. It has been a process to concede to this, to see it clearly and to release it over to God.

When my boys were small and they caught a cold, I didn't tell them that they didn't have a cold, we addressed it by resting, and drinking lots of water in between them blowing their nose. How many times do we encounter a setback, pretending that we are 100% and walk around like our nose isn't gushing out congestion? If we don't grab a tissue and expel nasal mucus, it won't be long until we drip all over the place. Having a cold, loss, a mishap or setback doesn't make us less or damaged, it makes us human.

Accepting ourselves and others is a process and a necessary task for a breakthrough. I believe that God loves ordinary people who trust him with an extraordinary humble heart. We all are God's beloved sons and daughters not because of our accomplishments or our achievements, we are God's beloved children because he chose us to come into the world to love him, sit with him, to be with him and to love him with all our hearts, souls and minds. When we can finally let go of all the facades and desires to impress each other, we are right sized and can recline into God's arms not needing to do a thing. We can breathe in and breathe out and let everything and everyone go. The show is over. The gig is up. Just like the singer-songwriter Jenn Johnson and Bethel music sings " A little longer" God would ask for our heart and our precious time, not our activities and diversions no, we don't have to do a thing, just be. All the bucket lists, dream boards and the to do lists can wait. God's love is like a hurricane, it sweeps us off our feet. His affection is all-consuming, wildly burning like a wildfire. He pours out his unconditional love and simply asks for our hearts, after all He gave us his. He gave us His very own life. Jesus experienced every human emotion that we have encountered or one day may. Betrayal, abandonment, rejection, hate, skepticism, fear, and the list goes on and on. He calls us to surrender all of it and to hold nothing back, setting down everything and everyone including ourselves dropping to His feet. We allow Him to have all of us not some parts but our whole self. His overwhelming radical and reckless devotion to us wraps us up like a familiar comfy blanket. God is a jealous God; He isn't interested in being second place. The first commandment was placed on the top for a reason, and I don't believe that it was by accident.

"Thou shalt have no other gods before me." God will wait on us to wake up and to dismantle all our idols and false gods. I believe that once we know this truth, we cannot unknow or deny this, we are immediately called to position Yahweh front and center now, not tomorrow when we get it all

together and stop our sinning and destructive habits, right this moment, we can pray, 'God I hand over to you, all of me, all of my traumas, dramas, wounded and secret places. I lay it all at Your feet and I won't let another second pass, in this very moment I abandon everything to be here with You."
 His outrageous love baths and showers us. His affection cascades over us more majestically than the outpouring of Niagara Falls. There will never be anyone who could ever care for us like our Daddy. Only the Lion of Judah could roar His power like strength and at the very same moment lay His life down like a gentle Lamb. His faithful hand takes ours and we sit and rest without checking the numbers on the clock or the phone by our side, all the distractions dim. It is just the two of us, alone.

Many of my friends know how fond I am of benches. Every time that I see one, I am reminded of reclining with Jesus. I don't care if the bench is in the middle of Times Square New York or beside a hiking trail in the middle of a forest in Montana or Michigan. I smile and if possible, sit for a moment, feeling God's presence. Who doesn't need to take a load off and relinquish all the meaningless nonsense we get caught up in at times? Perhaps your place may not be a bench, it may be your bedroom, church, temple, a park, the beach or a nature walk. It does not matter where or what, just that it involves being with Abba.

We all have our God moments, God encounters and "come to Jesus" moments. I want to end this devotional with a short story about coming to the end of myself and discovering how dearly loved I realized I was, am and always will be. It took a very long time for me to absorb and comprehend that God loves me, getting that truth from my head to my heart, and finally grasping how deep and wide His love is, was a process.

One morning I was sitting at the beach pouring out my heart to God about yet another major disappointment and loss in my life. Feeling utterly broken, unloved and no longer valued, I took a suggestion from my then counselor, Pastor Karen and read every single Brennan Manning book.

In the paperback that I was now pouring over, one of the chapters the author posed a life- changing question, I weep right now as I write it down.

"Imagine right this moment that Jesus walks in the door, comes up to you, looks you squarely in the eye and calls you by one word, what is that word?

What is the word that God knows you by? As I watched the waves move toward the shoreline in front of me and noticed some seagulls hovering and squawking above my head, I heard a small still voice say to me,

'Beloved Daughter.'

I began to repeat this a couple of times and once again I heard my Daddy's voice speak.

"Say it slower, Betty Jean."

I spoke it quietly and slowly, be loved daughter. Oh, my friend, I am recked in every way possible, and in my dismantled brokenness I am exposed to all of God's perfect wholeness. The Lord calls me by name, His beloved daughter, I am dearly loved. I believe that we are God's heartbeat and pulse, perhaps the very reason to continue earth and the world. One day this will all fade away. We will go home to our real refuge. Here and now, we get to walk with each other toward our eternal home which I believe bring us closer to Him every day. God keeps us all moving forward.

Most likely sometime between 2,000 and 10,000 B.C., the creator wiped everyone out except Noah, the only follower of God left on earth at that time. The wickedness, evil and destruction made God regret humankind and grieved His heart. But because of Noah's obedience to build the ark that would save him, his sons, wife, son's wives and two of every kind of creeping thing on Earth from the flood and torrential rain, we have God's promise that He will never again curse the ground because of humans, even though every inclination of the human heart is bent towards evil from his or her youth.

The Almighty made a covenant with Noah and to His sons that never again will a flood destroy the Earth. He gave a sign of his covenant for all generations to come. He placed a rainbow in the clouds, a banner as a token of a covenant between God, all of us and every living creature and the earth. I say all of this to simply remind us that God recognized Noah and he found grace in the eyes of the Lord. I am convinced that all is grace and favor. We simply come as we are, naked, exactly the way we came into the world, free of all our sensual appetites and dark secrets. We drop, throw or pry our fingers open one at a time watching the embers blow away and out of the ashes rises new life, a "do over."

Today may we start fresh and allow God's tender heart to meet ours, may we give Him all our soul.

Whether you are a ragamuffin, wounded soldier in the battlefield of life or an upright and righteous disciple, God is crazy about you, please just come as you are. God is dying to be with you and me, the love of the Father has covered and lavished us. It is God who calls us by name (Beloved daughter).
I am His and He is mine. He is yours and you are His beloved. Oh, Abba Father, we belong to You, there is no need to fear. There is only holy reverence and abounding love, and just as Jesus arose from the grave, we also rise out of our dying dark places and say thank you daddy, "thank you that we too are risen and alive!"

I glance down at my hand inside of His hand and through tears that well up and slide down my weathered cheek, I reach out my free hand and touch his nail scarred palm and see into the heart of

God, knowing like never that we are all so dearly loved.

What one or two words does God call you by?

Do you believe it?

How does that change your identity?

Where have you performed for God and others?

How do you feel knowing how dearly loved that you are?

Verses for the day: 1 John 3: 1 NIV

"See what great love the father has lavished on us, that we should be called children of God and that is what we are"!

Matthew 3: 17 KIV

"And lo a voice from heaven, saying this is my beloved son in whom I am well pleased."

Additional thoughts

Final thoughts

My heart and prayers are that you have been ministered to, by these words I penned with the help of our Father.

I believe He was the writer, and I was the vessel that He used to put pen to paper. I give the Lord all the credit, honor and glory for waking me up before sunrise many mornings with the anticipation to put thoughts and ideas into my writing journal to share with all of you.

Some of you I already know, and I love you. Others of you are friends I have not met just yet. In either case I prayed for you to pick up this devotional and to be blessed beyond measure as you read each word.

Thank you for being on my journey thus far and may we walk one another home towards Heaven, in love and service.

Final notes

Made in the USA
Columbia, SC
23 February 2024